MANCHESTER TRAMS

A Pictorial History of Manchester Road Transport

by

TED GRAY

A Memories publication

222 Kings Road
Firswood
Manchester
M16 0JW
Tel: 0161 862 9399

ISBN: 1 899181 86 5

Formerly published as
Manchester Trams (ISBN: 1899181 06 7)
& *Manchester Buses* (ISBN: 1 899181 10 5)

Design and layout by

‒Bill Hayes

Prepared by
Northern Publishing Services
28 Bedford Road, Firswood
Manchester, M16 0JA
Tel: 0161 862 9399

The Manchester Transport Museum Society

is a registered charity which was founded in 1961 by the late Clifford Taylor and others. Its members are volunteers who, with the support of Manchester City Council, established a Museum and tramway in Heaton Park in 1979. The MTMS seeks to preserve any items relevant to Manchester's tramways, and consequently holds an extensive archive section as well as numerous small exhibits. Temporarily stored elsewhere is an open-top double-deck Manchester tramcar, number 173. Several large items await restoration, including an example of an Eades Patent Reversible Horse-Tram from the Manchester Carriage & Tramways Company. The museum tramway operates on Sundays and Bank Holidays from Easter to the end of September, using tramcars from Manchester, Blackpool and Hull.

Printed by MFP Design & Print
Stretford, Manchester
Tel: 0161 864 4540

Front cover pictures: Two examples of Manchester transport rescued and cared for by volunteers. Single-deck tram 765, new in 1914, was restored by members of the Manchester Transport Museum Society, and now runs on a length of track in Heaton Park. Crossley bus 2150 (JN 791), dating from 1949, is one of several former Manchester vehicles preserved by the Greater Manchester Transport Society and displayed in the museum of Transport, Boyle Street, Cheetham Hill.
Back cover pictures: Front end views of tram 765 in Birchfields Road Depot and Leyland bus 3245 (JND 646) of 1951 outside the Museum in Boyle Street.

MANCHESTER TRAMS

A Pictorial History of the Tramways of Manchester

by

TED GRAY

&

ARTHUR KIRBY

INTRODUCTION

By an Act of 1875, the City of Manchester was empowered to construct tramway tracks along the main highways. The grooved, metal rails, sunk into the surface of the road, were designed to give passengers a smoother ride than was possible in horse-drawn omnibuses rattling over the cobbled streets. For the initial venture, Manchester joined forces with the County Borough of Salford, and the first line ran from Pendleton to Higher Broughton (Kersal Bar) by way of Manchester's Deansgate. Thus, both ends of the line were in Salford, with only the central section in Manchester. The Manchester length began at the city boundary at Albert Bridge (New Bailey Street) and led to Deansgate, thence outwards along Great Ducie Street, crossing the boundary once again at the Grove Inn on Bury New Road. In accordance with legislation in force at that time, the tracks had to be leased to private operators in return for an annual rent, usually fixed at 10% of the cost of construction.

John Greenwood of Pendleton had pioneered local horse-drawn omnibus services to Manchester's commercial centre in Market Street as early as 1824. His success had attracted competitors into the business, and by the 1850s services were offered along most of the main roads radiating from the city centre. In 1865 the various rivals merged their interests to form the Manchester Carriage Company. The Company then provided the public transport services throughout the Manchester area. In 1875, already having the necessary employees, stables, and workshops, and already operating the horse-bus services along the proposed tramway route, the Company was seen as the obvious lessee of the new tracks. However, disagreement arose between Manchester and the Company on the question of whether or not the Company should be obliged to rent *all* the tracks the Corporation saw fit to

construct, for additional lines were planned once the first route was complete. The Company had no wish to pay rent for lines which were likely to prove unprofitable, and therefore preferred to tender for each route separately. The Corporation, on the other hand, wanted the Company to rent the whole system, or nothing at all.

In the event, the lease was awarded to Messrs. Busby and Turton, carriage proprietors from Liverpool and Leeds respectively, promoters of tramways in several British towns. They adopted the title *'Manchester & Salford Tramways'*. Services began on the first section of the line on 18th May 1877. The lessees had ordered 30 tramway carriages from the Starbuck Company of Birkenhead, but from the outset, by some secret arrangement, the Carriage Company provided the staff, horse-power, depots and stables. In the 1877-80 period, additional lines were added and subsequently the lease was transferred, the operator's title being changed to *'The Manchester Carriage & Tramways Company'*.

The original lease was for a period of 21 years, and thus due to expire towards the turn of the century. By that time the 1870 Tramways Act had been amended to allow local authorities to work their own tramways if they so wished. The Company, not knowing whether its lease would be renewed, made offers of improvements and carried out experiments with electric and steam traction, ready to modernise its undertaking if its future was assured. However, the decision was taken not to renew the lease. Instead, the Company's empire was broken up, with many local authorities in the Greater Manchester area choosing to own and operate their own tramway services, using electric traction taking current from an overhead wire.

Salford purchased outright sufficient of the Company's assets as were required to work the horse-tram services in the Borough during the period of conversion, but Manchester allowed the Company to continue to operate routes until each was ready for electric traction. The official opening of Manchester's first electric tramcar route, Albert Square to Cheetham Hill, was on 6th June 1901, with public services beginning on the following day. Thereafter, the number of electric tramway routes expanded, and the tramcar was in the ascendancy until threatened by the proliferation of motor bus services in the late-1920s. Tramway services declined as many were converted to motor bus operation in the 1930s, and the last Corporation tramcar ran in Manchester on the 10th January 1949.

In 1992 trams returned to Manchester via the first phase of the Metrolink system, which, though principally a railway service, has 1.73 kilometres of street-level track in the city centre, linking the former electric railway routes to Bury and Altrincham. There is also a 0.7 kilometre branch to Piccadilly *Undercroft* – i.e. under Piccadilly (formerly London Road) railway station. Further extensions are planned, and the city centre street section will remain common to all future routes.

ACKNOWLEDGEMENTS

For a pictorial history such as this, credit must be accorded to those photographers, known and unknown, who faithfully captured the local scene. Many of the illustrations are from the files of the former Manchester Corporation Transport Department (MCT), others are the work of early commercial postcard publishers. In the 1930s and '40s, a number of tramway enthusiasts set out to capture the declining years of tramway operation, and readily gave permission for their pictures to be reproduced. In many cases, their work is preserved today by bodies such as the Tramway Museum Society, the Greater Manchester Transport Society, and the Manchester Transport Museum Society (MTMS). Photographers to whom we are indebted include A.M.Gunn, and the late W.A.Camwell, W.Gratwicke, R.B.Parr, and G.N.Southerden. Illustrations are individually acknowledged where the photographer is known, and apologies are offered for any inadvertent omissions. For the MTMS, the work of the late Ray Dunning in seeking out and preserving items of Manchester's transport history is gratefully acknowledged. John Howarth of Eccles kindly assisted with the provision of a number of timetable advertisements from the 1930s. Details of the tramcar fleet have been extracted from data compiled by F.P.Groves, and printed in I.A.Yearsley's book listed below, a comprehensive volume which is acknowledged as the source of much general information.

By the 1890s the Manchester Carriage & Tramways Company operated over 500 horse-drawn tramcars on some 75 miles of track in and around the city. Most were of the Eades Patent Reversible type. Shorter and lighter than the original double-ended cars, the Eades cars were cheaper to build, required only one staircase, and needed fewer horses and less depot space. On reaching outer termini, a reversible car could swivel on its truck, obviating the need to unhitch the horses. In the city centre, routes were arranged to pass around terminal loops so that they did not need to swivel in the busy streets. The cars were built at the Company's Pendleton Works, where inventor John Eades was Manager. Most Eades cars could seat 41, 18 on longitudonal benches inside and 23 on top. In this example from the Openshaw route, a fare table hangs in the lower saloon window, listing the penny stages. Until 1888 the standard fare was threepence, but thereafter short-distance fares were introduced. It also became cheaper to travel *outside* (i.e. on the open top) than inside. Tickets were not issued in Company days, nor were there any fixed stops for boarding or alighting, though it was not thought proper to halt a car on an incline where the horses might have difficulty in re-starting.

PHOTO: MCT

The 21-year leases of additional routes opened in the 1877-79 period were extended so that all expired on the 27th April 1901. By arrangement with the Carriage Company, the construction of the replacement track for the heavier electric cars, and the erection of overhead equipment, was able to commence before the expiry date. This example of an electric tramway junction is at Market Street/Cross Street. The rails are fixed on a bed of concrete, but the granite setts have yet to be replaced. A burden placed upon tramways by the 1870 Act was a requirement to pave and maintain the roadway between, and for 18 inches on either side of the rails. In 1870 it had been argued that the tram horses would wear out the stone setts, but, incredibly, this particular clause was never repealed, even though the electric tramcars made no use whatsoever of the road surface. Tramway operators were thus obliged to maintain considerable areas of the main streets for the benefit of others, including ultimately their motor-bus competitors.

In 1899 Manchester took delivery of six sample electric tramcars (five double-deck, one four-wheel single-deck) in order to assess their various merits before placing orders. One of the sample cars was constructed by John Eades at Pendleton. His son, also John, was appointed first Manager of the Manchester Corporation Car Works. It was considered that some 430 vehicles would be needed for delivery in the period 1901-03, the majority being of the four-wheel double-deck type. However, the total eventually included 100 double-deck and 25 single-deck bogie cars. Orders were split between the firms of G.F.Milnes and Brush. Car 331 is an example of the Milnes product. Fleet numbering began with car 101, the Eades sample car.

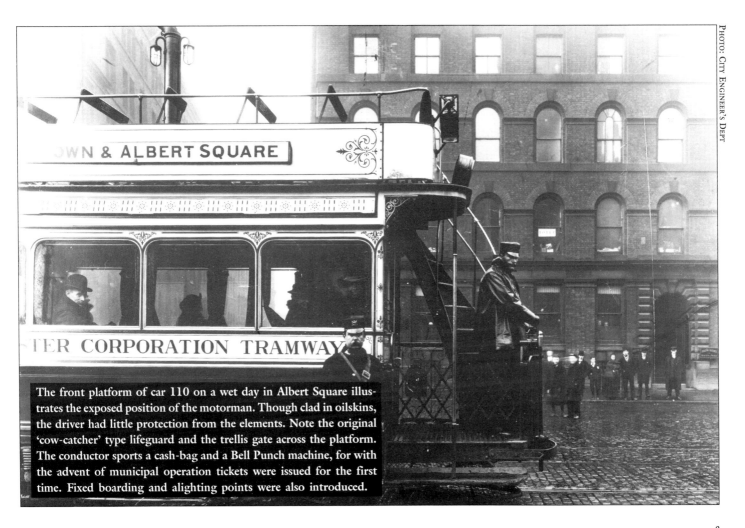

OWN & ALBERT SQUARE

TER CORPORATION TRAMWAY

The front platform of car 110 on a wet day in Albert Square illustrates the exposed position of the motorman. Though clad in oilskins, the driver had little protection from the elements. Note the original 'cow-catcher' type lifeguard and the trellis gate across the platform. The conductor sports a cash-bag and a Bell Punch machine, for with the advent of municipal operation tickets were issued for the first time. Fixed boarding and alighting points were also introduced.

PHOTO: MRS. F. GREENWAY

◀ During the period of conversion from horse-drawn to electric operation it was possible to see both forms of traction side-by-side in the city centre. In this 1902 view of the Market Street/Cross Street junction a Cheetham Hill-bound electric tramcar approaches from Albert Square, whilst horse-trams for Old Trafford and Brooks' Bar move towards Piccadilly.

▶ Deansgate in 1901-02 with car 298 ready to depart for the Grove Inn. Until June 1903, Salford cars were debarred from Deansgate because of a failure to agree inter-running arrangements. In retaliation, Manchester cars could run along Bury New Road only as far as the municipal boundary at the Grove Inn. To maintain services in the other direction, from Deansgate to the Salford boundary at Regent Bridge, Manchester purchased 11 redundant horse-trams and 132 horses, with temporary stabling and depot accommodation in Elm Street, off Water Street.

Photo: MCT

Manchester's first depot for electric tramcars was at Queens Road, Cheetham Hill, designed to house 252 vehicles on 42 six-car tracks which fanned at right-angles from the approach line. Notices fixed to the pillars indicated storage tracks for particular routes. Nearest to the camera is the 'REPAIR BAY.' The first section of Hyde Road Depot and Works, needed to house and maintain the large number of cars already on order, was in use by December 1902, but the full complex was not completed until 1905. Additional tramcar depots were subsequently constructed at Princess Road (1909) and Birchfields Road (1928).

A notice from the 1904 timetable, in which the word *'buses'* refers to horse-drawn omnibuses.

MANCHESTER CORPORATION TRAMWAYS.

Chorlton=cum=Hardy.

Buses run regularly between MOSS SIDE (Prince of Wales Hotel) and CHORLTON GREEN via Upper Chorlton Road.

CHEADLE, DIDSBURY & PALATINE RD.

A few horse-drawn omnibuses were retained from the Carriage Company in order to provide services to Chorlton, Cheadle and Northenden, areas where it had not been thought worthwhile to construct tramways, or where construction was pending. These were housed at the Chorlton Road shed, as seen here. Three Crossley motor buses were acquired in 1906 to replace horse-buses, but after protests, the horse-drawn vehicles were re-instated and appear to have remained in use until 1915. One example was preserved, and is now on display in the Museum of Transport, Cheetham Hill.

▲ From their beginnings in 1901 Manchester's electric tramways expanded to reach Ashton, Denton, Middleton, Oldham, Sale, Stockport, Stretford, and Trafford Park. In 1905-06 over 133 million passengers were carried. With the extension to Altrincham in 1907, the system was substantially complete. Most main roads had a tramway. In the days before traffic congestion, tracks were constructed in the centre of the roadway, the overhead wires often being supported by ornate poles, as seen here in Cheetham Hill Village. As the number of vehicles competing for road space increased, the centre standards became a hazard and began to be removed about 1909 in favour of side poles mounted on the pavement.

◄ Piccadilly in 1904, then as now, had its tangle of overhead wires, a necessary proliferation at an important tramway junction. Milnes car 298, on the Conran Street route, sports a new roller blind destination indicator, which extended a car's availability for different routes, though the tram in front still retains the more restrictive four-sided rotating box device. The Milnes cars were easily identifiable by the cut-away dash near the brake staff. White tops were fitted to staff caps on May 1st each year.

As services increased, additional double-deck cars were ordered, and in 1903 the first 25 single-deck bogie cars were delivered, numbered 512-536. They were intended for routes having restricted clearances under low railway bridges. The opening of various sections of track linking Queens Road (Cheetham Hill Road) with Seymour Grove by way of Belle Vue and Brooks's Bar, evolved into the circuitous '53' route. This avoided the city centre, and was known as the *'circular route,'* but, in fact, it was considerably short of a full circle. The route used a portion of Wilmslow Road, where car 524 is seen passing double-deck car 206. The letter 'D' on car 206 was an early attempt to display route information, for service numbers were not introduced until 1914.

By 1906 the 'circular route' was so busy that 35 tramcars were needed for its operation, a total achieved only by temporarily removing upper-deck seats and fittings from 12 double-deck cars. Consequently, 20 more single-deck cars were purchased, numbered 649-668. Car 666 is seen in later years about to pass under the low bridge in Stanley Grove, Longsight, clearly demonstrating the reason why the route was unsuitable for double-deck cars.

In 1905 the Tramways Department began a parcels service, guaranteeing a same-day delivery in the city provided the package was handed-in before 3.45 p.m. Items could be handed to the crew of any service car, who transferred them at one of several collection offices established around the town. Special parcels cars ran between these offices several times a day, and the final delivery was made by a boy with a handcart. There were seven cars with van-type bodies for the parcels department. Car 6 was photographed in 1906 by The Polygon, Bury Old Road, on a delivery run to the Cheetham Hill office.

◀ (FAR LEFT) The unpopularity of the open top-deck in wet weather led to consideration of the fitting of top-covers. The first experiments took place in 1904, the construction of the *'balloon'* roof being designed to fit on existing tramcars without the need for reconstruction of the bodywork. The top-cover fixed on car 589 was deemed to be the most suitable, and approval was given for similar roofs to be manufactured in Hyde Road Works.

◀ (LEFT) The 'balloon' covers were fitted to 50 existing cars and to the 50 new bogie cars (599-648) being delivered in 1905-06 from the Brush Company. The platform design adopted for Manchester cars was such that it would have been difficult to extend the roof to shield the staircase, or the canopy to protect the driver, without major and expensive alterations. The 90-degree turn of the staircase and the exposed position of the controls may be noted in this view of car 636.

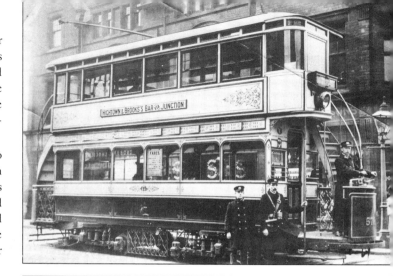

▶ (TOP RIGHT) The crew of 'balloon' car 578 pose proudly for the photographer at the Hightown terminus, ready to return on the cross-city route to Brooks's Bar via Junction, the latter being a spot in Hulme with a public house of that name. The third member of crew, the trolley boy, was a luxury seemingly indulged only by Manchester and Salford. Originally devised to combat unemployment amongst the young, the appointment proved to be a training-ground for future guards and drivers. Duties included the supervision of boarding and alighting passengers, bell signals, destination displays, and, of course, turning the trolley at termini.

▶ (BOTTOM RIGHT) The long route to Altrincham opened in 1907. 'Balloon' car 626 stands at the end of the line, trolley turned ready for its journey back to Manchester. Note the cast-iron horse-trough and the drinking fountain, once common sights at major junctions. The cab horse enjoys his fodder in a slack period.

SPECIAL CAR

89

701

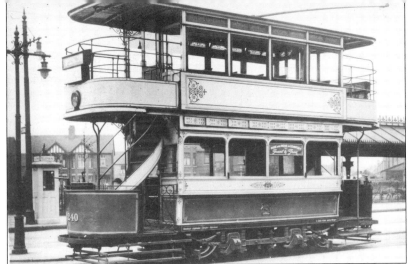

▲ After completing the 'balloon' top-covers for the bogie cars, attention turned to the question of similar treatment for the smaller cars. To give protection to those passengers who preferred to travel in the open air, a balcony-type cover was favoured. This time the conversion was much more thorough, involving the provision of longer platforms, new 180-degree staircases, and extended canopies, which latter alteration also increased the seating capacity. Some 95 four-wheel cars were so altered in the 1906-08 period, and orders were given for a similar design of top-cover for 25 bogie cars.

◄ In 1909 the Hyde Road Works commenced a three-year programme of building complete tramcar bodies, 11 four-wheelers (669-679) and 38 large bogie-cars (680-717). All were designed to have top-covers of the balcony type. With the introduction of route numbers in 1914, car 701 was the recipient of an experimental stencil-plate holder, adorned with wrought-iron surrounds. Evidently the circular design was not approved, possibly because it was more difficult to store and issue the plates, for it was discarded in favour of the rectangular pattern.

▶ (RIGHT) Car 510, originally a Milnes open-top car of 1903, is shown as rebuilt with canopy top-cover and sporting the more usual type of service number, mounted immediately below the destination indicator. The provision of service numbers supplemented the route information carried on boards mounted on the top-deck sides.

▶ (FAR RIGHT) Appointments to the traffic staff were exclusively male until well into the First World War, when so many men having joined the forces, conductresses were employed for the first time. The ladies were not universally welcomed - many thought they were taking the jobs of those who had enlisted, and demanded that they be dismissed as soon as the men returned from the war. A young 'clippie' poses with the motorman on car 731, a single-truck car new in 1913.

PHOTO: MCT

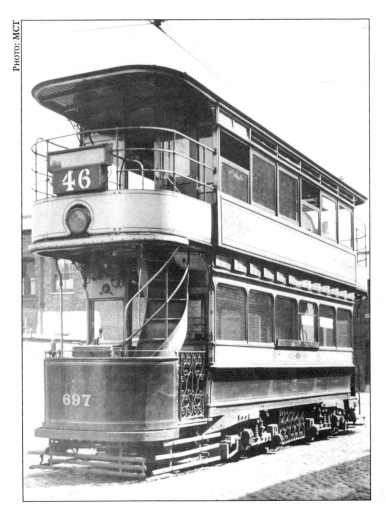

◄ One of the large bogie-cars, number 697, built at Hyde Road in 1911-12, mounted on Brush 22E trucks, and fitted with British Thomson-Houston electrical equipment, stands in Bowes Street at the side of Princess Road Depot. On cars built after mid-1913, the position of the headlamp was changed from the top-deck end to the middle of the platform dash-plate.

◄ In 1901-03 the earliest cars had been equipped with the 'cow-catcher' type wire mesh lifeguard, but these were replaced and all subsequent additions to the fleet were fitted with a locally-produced device. The Hudson & Bowring lifeguard consisted of a swinging gate which, when meeting an obstruction, cut off power and caused a tray to drop on to the track. Spaces between the side bogies were protected by wrought-iron 'dog gates.'

Manchester's first totally-enclosed tramcar was a 1919 rebuild of one of the 40 remaining open-top bogie-cars. The rebuild incorporated vestibules round both the platforms and top-deck-ends. After inspection, it was decided that all future new cars and all rebuilds would be to a similar pattern, giving a distinctive 'Manchester' style. More cars were converted to this design, one of the earliest in 1919-20 being number 198, seen here on the left in this view of Oxford Street in the 1920s.

PHOTO: NATIONAL RAILWAY MUSEUM

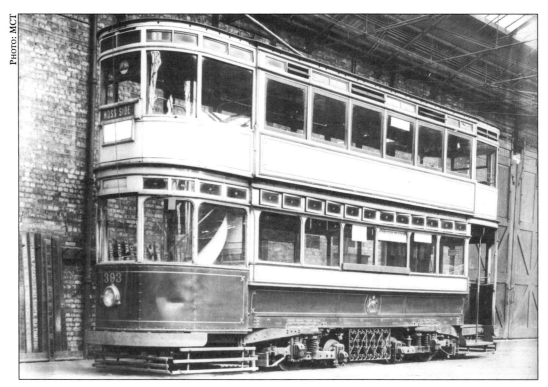

Photo: MCT

In the post-war years, more new bogie-cars were ordered from the English Electric Company. In addition, the Hyde Road Car Works continued to construct bodies. All were mounted on Brush 22E trucks. The fleet totalled over 800 vehicles by 1922. However, the earliest members of the fleet were by then over 20 years old, and some were in poor condition. The first replacement car, as distinct from a rebuild, was car 393, dating from March 1924. Similar in appearance to the new cars being turned out from the Hyde Road Works since 1920, the lower deck was new, but the top-deck was a flat-roof rebuild of the cover removed from the original single-truck car 393, but with an extra portion spliced-in to give additional length. More replacement cars of the same type followed in 1924-26. They were given the fleet numbers of withdrawn cars. Note (left) the route boards propped in racks against the wall.

PHOTO: CITY ENGINEER'S DEPT

Princess Road Car Shed in April 1926 shows a preponderance of the all-enclosed bogie-cars which became the mainstay of the fleet. The difference between the flat and curved-roof cars may be noted. The fourth car from the right is number 373, one of 19 single-truck balcony cars which were given vestibules in the 1921-24 period.

PHOTO: W. A. CAMWELL

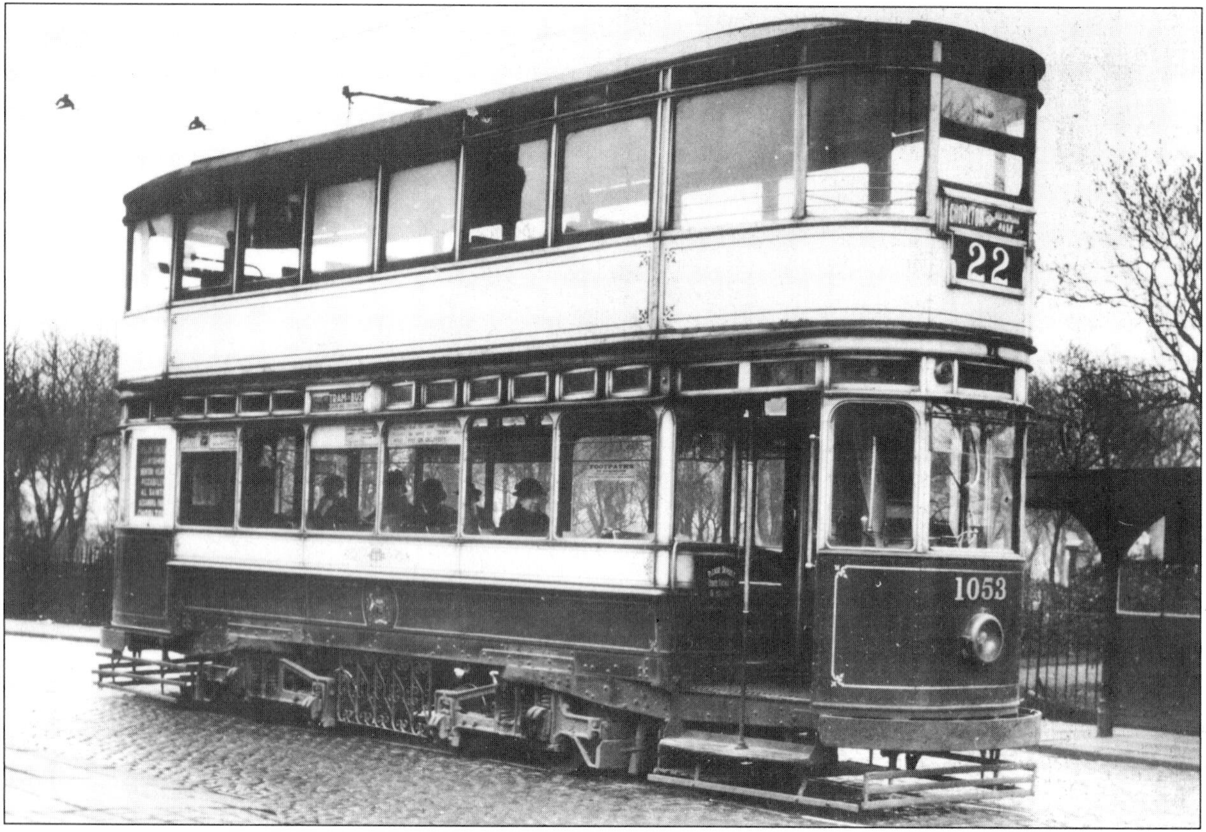

The highest fleet number carried by a Manchester car was 1053, the last of a batch of 50 new vehicles delivered in 1927-28 from the English Electric Company. By that date, all the remaining open-top cars had been covered or withdrawn. There were still some 400 unvestibuled balcony and 'balloon' cars, but their combined total was now exceeded by the number of all-enclosed vehicles. Car 1053 is seen at Moston in 1937, ready to return on route 22 to Chorlton.

PHOTO: MCT

The last replacement cars constructed in the Hyde Road Works were fitted with wooden reversible transverse seats in the lower saloon, replacing the traditional longitudonal benches of earlier years. (INSET) Note the two-and-one arrangement, necessitating an off-set gangway, the ruby-coloured quarter lights, and the lampshades.

▲ The Hyde Road Car Works continued to construct replacement cars throughout the 1920s. In this 1929 view along 'The Avenue,' the bodies of car 797 and others are stored on trestles at right-angles to those in the repair shop. To the left were the truck and machine shops, brass foundry, smithy and electrical department.

◄ The overhead travelling crane was able to lift and move complete tramcars. Car 806 is seen under lift.

▲ As the number of motor vehicles grew, there was a proposal to relieve congestion by excluding tramcars from the city centre. The Tramways Committee understandably opposed such a suggestion. Piccadilly, decorated for the Civic Week celebrations in October 1926, gives some impression of the dramatic effect such a ban might have had. Amongst the Manchester cars are two Salford vehicles operating on the joint routes from Levenshulme to Kersal and Prestwich, the first of which had begun at the end of August 1926.

▼ In the suburbs, plans for rapid transit were realised to some extent by the provision of long stretches of reserved track on Princess Road (1925) and Kingsway (1926), single centre poles returning to fashion to hold up both wires. On the reserved tracks the tramcars were able to proceed speedily, unimpeded by other road traffic. Sadly, such provision was not possible in the crowded streets of central Manchester. In this mid-1930s view of Kingsway, the almost complete absence of motor vehicles makes the reserved track seem unnecessary for car 498 as it heads for East Didsbury.

SPECIAL CAR
20

266

◀R. Stuart Pilcher was appointed General Manager in 1929, becoming responsible for a fleet at maximum of 952 tramcars. The programme for 21 further replacement bogie-cars and 8 rebuilds was continued in 1929-30, the latest having the luxury of upholstered seats in the lower saloon. Pilcher, favouring the single-truck high-speed car, then switched to the construction of 38 four-wheel 'Pullman' cars in 1930-32. These replaced (and took the fleet numbers of) some withdrawn cars. Older cars, mainly of the balcony type, were being scrapped at this time, and most of the single-deck cars were withdrawn in 1930 on the conversion of the 53 route to bus operation. The new 'Pilcher' cars had a long wheelbase, with small wheels, high-speed motors, and a low-slung body. Having magnetic track brakes, the new cars were especially suitable for hilly routes. Car 266 was the first of the type to appear in service in May 1930.

PHOTO: G. N. SOUTHERDEN

A number of the single-truck open-ended cars survived into the 1930s. In 1932 car 152 was captured working the shuttle service between Ashton and Denton. Note the unusual destination display. Evidently, DENTON did not appear on this particular roller blind, and the destination is shown on a printed card placed between the glass and the blind.

PHOTO: MCT

The parcels service continued, although in the 1930s the work was often carried out by motor van. Even so, firms wishing to have parcels collected continued to display a sign which read 'TRAM' long after tramcars had ceased to be used. In this picture at Chorlton, a parcel is being handed to the conductor of car 807 for transfer to the sorting office. Another useful public service performed by the tramcars was the late evening collection of mail via a letter box on the 'Post Car,' inward-bound on most routes at about 9.00 p.m. On reaching the city centre, the post-boxes were tranferred to the main Post Office.

The platform of car 872 shows a typical use of the under-stair resistance box – a convenient shelf on which to place the ticket box, and a useful spot to keep the brew can warm.

Well-used rails in the busy city centre were subject to greater wear than those in the outskirts, and consequently needed renewing more frequently. Before a major junction was relaid, it was the practice to set out the rails and points in the Bennett Street Permanent Way Yard, in order to check that everything would fit before digging up the street surface. This was the new November 1934 layout for St. Peter's Square.

▲ An oddity in the Manchester fleet was tram 436, converted in 1923 from its original open-top condition to a one-man-operated car, with front-exits located on the nearside (i.e. by the driver). It was used on the Stockport Road-Wilmslow Road shuttle service along Rusholme High Street.

◄The driver of car 891 stands on the fender as he fixes the trolley-rope in Piccadilly. There were various devices designed to prevent the trolley flying up in the case of a dewirement. One such was the 'trolley retriever,' a spring-loaded cylindrical drum on the end of the rope, which fitted into a socket on the dash-plate and kept the rope taut. Retrievers were tried in both Manchester and Salford, but fell into disuse. In the end, nothing was better than fastening the rope to some suitable platform stanchion or bar – the rope had to remain slack to allow for side-to-side swinging of the pole on curves.

The Piccadilly end of Market Street on a wet day in 1934 has a line of five all-enclosed cars waiting opposite Lewis's department store for the High Street junction traffic lights to change in their favour. Two horse-drawn carts are in evidence, but the number of private motor vehicles using city-centre streets is beginning to escalate.

PHOTO: MANCHESTER EVENING NEWS

A 1935 picture looks down on the junction of Market Street and Cross Street. Traffic moving into Corporation Street (left) appears to be at a standstill. Amongst the vehicles is one L.M.S.Railway house-removal container on a horse-drawn cart; a motor lorry carrying an alarming pile of sacks; and a cart advertising *'Westmacott's Quinine Champagne.'* Would the latter two infringe today's safety and trade description regulations? Car 398 waits to advance to the Exchange terminus of route 19, the guard having already turned his indicator to 'HYDE' for the reverse journey. Behind it is a tramcar of Stockport Corporation on joint route 35.

◄ A page from the 1936 timetable advertises the one-shilling 'Cheap Travel' Ticket, offering unlimited travel for a whole day. On jointly-operated routes, the ticket was valid only for the Manchester portion. By the mid-1930s more routes had been converted to motor bus operation, and the number of trams remaining totalled 755 in March 1936.

► A press photograph dated 20th April 1936 was taken to show freak darkness at mid-day. Car 113, followed by 832, moves along Cross Street with lights ablaze. Note the wooden indicator arm, hand-operated by the driver to warn of left turns, or the guard at the rear for right turns. These primitive trafficator signals were not fitted to all cars. The arms were not readily visible to traffic approaching alongside, and were easily broken. Most became disused.

PHOTO: MANCHESTER EVENING NEWS

Tramway tracks in Manchester were usually double throughout. However, narrow streets in certain parts of Moss Side necessitated a single-track one-way system or, alternatively, single track with passing loops, as on Lloyd Street South.

▶ Joint workings brought Manchester trams into contact with those of other operators on several parts of the system. At Hyde Market Place Manchester car 424 working on route 19 waits with Stalybridge, Hyde, Mossley & Dukinfield "green linnet" car 63. The open-ended SHMD car is ready to return to Stockport (Edgeley). It has a fitting for a Manchester-style route number stencil, for until late-1935 SHMD cars shared in the operation of route 19.

◀ Other joint workings were to be seen on the two routes to Ashton-Under-Lyne. Pilcher car 274 leaves Ashton centre in 1932 on route 26 to Manchester (Stevenson Square via Ashton New Road and Droylsden), whilst Ashton car 12 arrives on a local service. The second Manchester-Ashton route (number 28) was to Piccadilly via Fairfield and Ashton Old Road. The Ashton blue contrasted with Manchester's red livery. In March 1938 trolley-buses took over operation of the Manchester-Ashton service, and Ashton's few remaining trams were scrapped.

37

PHOTO: A. M. GUNN

◀ Manchester Pilcher car 104 passes Oldham 125 on the hilly Waterhead section in August 1935.

PHOTO: W. A. CAMWELL

▶Stockport's Mersey Square is the setting as Stockport 23 and Manchester 1035 wait to set off on their respective journeys. A large black letter 'H' painted on the dash of some Stockport cars indicated that they were low enough to pass under the bridges on the Hyde route. It was relatively unusual to see a service number displayed on a Stockport tram, but this one has the number 2 hanging in the top-deck end window. Stockport was the last town in the Greater Manchester area to abandon its trams. Some routes survived until August 1951.

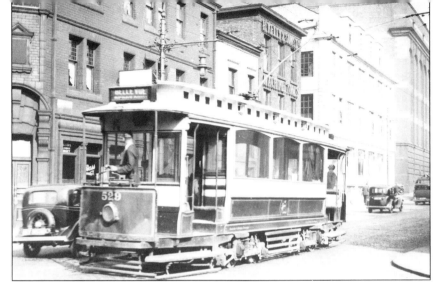

PHOTO: A. M. GUNN

◀ In 1925 the Middleton Electric Traction Company was taken over jointly by the Corporations of Manchester, Oldham and Rochdale, as a result of which Manchester acquired ten 1902 single-deck bogie cars, similar to the ones used on the 53 route. After some modification and reconditioning, six entered service as numbers 994-999 and one as 529, taking the fleet number of a withdrawn car. Three were scrapped. Car 529 survived the demise of the 53 route in 1930 to remain in use carrying bags of dried sand between depots until 1938. It is seen in Miller Street in 1937.

▶ A 1938 view of the three-track layout in Piccadilly, looking towards Market Street, includes a Stockport car and a new bus turning out of Portland Street. By this date, trolley-bus wires mingled with the tramway overhead, and the direction of travel on the centre track had been reversed to make it available for cars moving towards London Road. Note the clock on the facade of the Transport Offices at 55 Piccadilly.

PHOTO: MCT

PHOTO: MANCHESTER GUARDIAN

PHOTO: OLDHAM EVENING CHRONICLE

▲ An unidentified Pilcher car braves the snow in Oldham on route 20 to Waterhead. Though the destination is obscured, someone has recently had a finger on the lamp, where 'OXO' stands out clearly!

◄ Pilcher car 266 threads through the Market Street shoppers as it turns into Cross Street about 1936. The destination is misleading. It is possible that the car was entering service on route 11A, Heaton Park to Alexandra Park via Albert Square. Car 253 behind displays a 37 black-on-white paper route number, a reverse of the usual stencil.

PHOTO: DAILY HERALD

In June 1938 problems of increasing congestion led to the introduction of a one-way traffic system between All Saints and the city centre. Inward-bound cars approached via Oxford Road, whilst outward cars left the city via Princess Street. The effect was to double the number of tramcars and halve the length of available track on these streets. In this rush-hour picture, the line of trams waiting to move along Oxford Road stretches back as far as All Saints, but the private cars are able to overtake easily by straddling the unused outward track. The one-way scheme resulted in disruption of the tramcar timetables, and further advanced the argument in favour of conversion to the more versatile motor bus. This was the last year in which the balcony cars appeared in service, and the General Manager proposed complete abandonment of the tramways within three years.

Tramcar drivers were not the only persons confused on the introduction of the new one-way scheme. At All Saints, police officers were on duty to advise motorists. Three tramcars wait to move out from Grosvenor Street.

PHOTO: D.KOURKE

▲ Tramcar withdrawals accelerated in the late 1930s as more routes were converted to motor bus operation. A June 1939 view at Chorlton terminus shows the rear of a newly-delivered Crossley 'Mancunian' bus. Trams 327 on route 23 (Chorlton-Hollinwood) and 1021 on the 37 (Southern Cemetery-Levenshulme) are working on two of the few remaining tram services. Route 23 was, in fact, converted in July of that year, but re-instated as a wartime measure in 1940.

▼ In the 1939-45 War ladies were employed once again out on the road as traffic staff. The majority were conductresses on buses, trolley-buses, and trams, but a few were trained as tram drivers.

PHOTO: MCT

By September 1939, only 450 trams remained, and had the abandonment programme continued, all would have gone within 18 months. Wartime shortages of fuel brought a temporary reprieve, however. Car 1018 outside Birchfields Road Depot displays the white fenders and headlamp mask required by the blackout regulations.

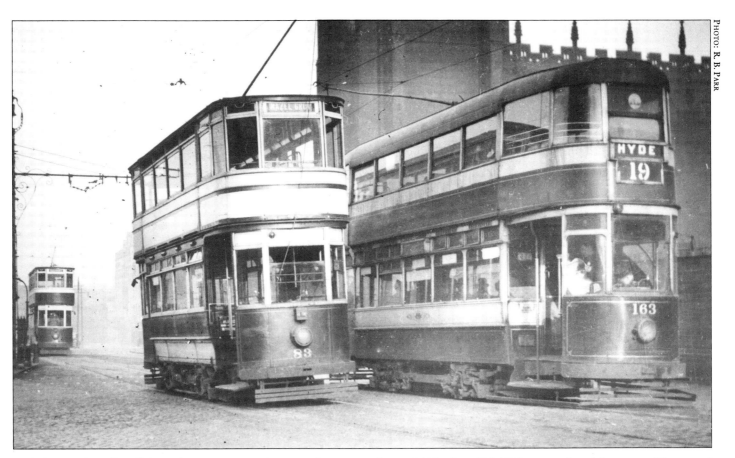

PHOTO: R. B. PARR

With the cessation of hostilities, and as soon as motor bus manufacturers could return to peacetime production, the tramway abandonment programme was resumed. Oldham's tramways closed completely in August 1946, after which Pilcher cars released from route 20 appeared mainly on route 19 to Hyde. In this December 1946 view car 163 shares the Exchange terminus with two Stockport cars.

▲ Manchester's last trams ran on the peak-hour Levenshulme service on the morning of 10th January 1949, after which there was a ceremonial procession from Piccadilly to Birchfields Road Depot. Employees gather round car 1007 in the depot. Through its windows can be seen the new Crossley buses which replaced the trams on the services to Levenshulme and Stockport.

▶ An ignominious end for Manchester trams. After the removal of any re-saleable material, withdrawn trams were scrapped in Hyde Road Yard. The exceptions were the 38 Pilcher cars, which were advertised for sale in 1946. All saw further service elsewhere, and all had left Manchester before the final days of tramway operation. Leeds bought 7, Sunderland 6, Edinburgh 11, and Aberdeen 14. The last two undertakings had previously been managed by R. Stuart Pilcher.

MANCHESTER CORPORATION TRAMWAYS: ROUTE DETAILS

Compiled by A. K. Kirby

Route numbers were not introduced until May 1914. However, for the purposes of this table, the earliest service along all or part of the route has been noted alongside the number eventually allocated. Numbers under 10 were not used ; numbers from 61 upwards were allocated to Salford, where they were not used until 1926. Many routes were subject to alteration from time to time, being lengthened, shortened, amended or absorbed as traffic required. Short-workings and variations were denoted by suffixes, 27H being the furthest letter reached in the alphabet. Dates of first and last **full day** of regular operation by tram are given. Several routes, or sections of them, continued to see part-day peak-period workings by tram after the date quoted. For example, workmen's services into Trafford Park continued until 24-8-1946, long after the regular tram service had ceased. Similarly, because of wartime conditions in the 1939-45 period, certain routes (for example, 13, 23, 38, 42F), or sections of them, were revived and returned to operation by tram.

ROUTE		FIRST DAY	LAST FULL DAY AND ROUTE
	Deansgate-Grove Inn (Bury New Road)	28-6-1901	30-4-1903	Grove Inn-Deansgate-Regent Bridge *(Incorporated in a Salford route)*
10	Hightown-Deansgate via Waterloo Road	30-9-1901	3-9-1938	Cheetham Hill Road-Chorlton
11	Cheetham Hill (Crescent Rd)-Albert Square	7-6-1901	4-7-1937	Heaton Park (Bury Old Road)-Alexandra Park
12	Hightown-Albert Square	7-6-1901	5-3-1939	Hightown-Greenheys
13	Hightown-Albert Square	7-6-1901	11-6-1939	Hightown-Chorlton
14	Singleton Rd-Albert Square via Cheetham Hill	18-5-1902	17-7-1926	Heaton Park-Albert Square
15	Heaton Park (Middleton Rd)-Albert Square	1-4-1904	18-11-1934	Greenheys-Middleton Road
16	Middleton-Middleton Junction via Oldham Rd	21-9-1903	31-3-1935	*(Merged with bus 54 to Stevenson Square)*
17	Blackley (Polefield Rd)-High Street	5-7-1901	12-11-1932	Rochdale-High Street *(joint)*
18	Blackley-High Street	5-7-1901	1-5-1934	Heywood-High Street
19	Denton-Piccadilly	1-6-1902	14-3-1948	Hyde (Broomstair Bridge)-Exchange Station
20	Waterhead-Piccadilly *(joint with Oldham)*	21-1-1907	3-8-1946	Waterhead-Piccadilly
21	Hollinwood-Piccadilly	1-4-1903	15-2-1931	Hollinwood-Stevenson Square
22	Piccadilly-Alexandra Park via City Rd	1-12-1902	27-3-1938	Moston Cemetery-Chorlton
23	Piccadilly-Alexandra Park	1-12-1902	1-7-1939	Hollinwood-Chorlton *(Reinstated 27.5.40-11.2.45)*

ROUTE		FIRST DAY	LAST FULL DAY AND ROUTE	
24	Kenyon Lane (Lightbowne Rd)-Oldham Road	7-3-1904	7-3-1937	Moston Cemetery-Stevenson Square
25	Bradford Road-Piccadilly	22-10-1903	26-10-1930	Hulme Hall Lane-Stevenson Square
26	Audenshaw (Snipe Inn)-Piccadilly	1-4-1903	30-7-1938	Audenshaw-Stevenson Square (as 26B)
27	Piccadilly-Old Trafford (near Seymour Grove)	9-3-1903	30-7-1938	Droylsden-Old Trafford
28	Audenshaw (Snipe Inn)-Piccadilly (George Street)	1-4-1903	1-3-1938	Ashton-Piccadilly
29	Stretford Road-All Saints	1-12-1902	17-2-1934	Trafford Park-Fairfield
30	Guide Bridge-Trafford Park	16-12-1908	4(?)-1-1936	Fairfield-Trafford Bridge
31	Fairfield Wells-Piccadilly	31-10-1904	19-3-1938	Fairfield-Chorlton
32	Clowes Street (Hyde Road)-Exchange Station	1-6-1902	17-2-1946	Reddish-Exchange Station, via Clowes Street
33	Denton-Haughton Green	7-10-1903		*(Absorbed into route 57 23-7-1923)*
33	Reddish-Swinton *(joint with Salford)*	19-9-1926	1-2-1948	Reddish (Bull's Head)-Victoria Street
34	Belle Vue-Exchange Station	1-6-1902		*(Absorbed into joint route 34 below)*
34	Belle Vue-Weaste *(joint with Salford)*	3-10-1926	24-7-1937	Belle Vue-Weaste *(joint)*
35	Piccadilly (George St)-Stockport (Heaton Lane)	1-6-1902	9-1-1949	Exchange Station-Hazel Grove
35B	Albert Square-Stockport (Mersey Square)	30-7-1922	15-2-1948	Albert Square-Stockport
36	Exchange Station-Heaton Chapel	2-8-1904		*(See joint route below)*
36	Levenshulme-Kersal *(joint with Salford)*	5-9-1926	1-6-1947	Albert Square-Southern Cemetery
37	Exchange Station-Levenshulme (Albert Road)	1-6-1902		*(Absorbed into joint route below)*
37	Levenshulme-Prestwich *(joint with Salford)*	29-8-1926	3-10-1948	St. Mary's Gate-Levenshulme
38	Longsight-Albert Square (via Plymouth Grove)	30-6-1902	3-9-1938	Albert Square-Chorlton
39	Stockport Road-Wilmslow Road	1-10-1906	14-5-1939	*(Un-numbered from 16-1-1933; see below)*
39	East Didsbury-Exchange Station (ex-37B)	16-1-1933	14-7-1946	East Didsbury-Exchange Station
40	Victoria Park-Hightown	19-4-1902	2-2-1947	East Didsbury-Albert Square
41	W.Didsbury-Royal Exchange (in via Albert Square)	1-12-1902	4-12-1938	West Didsbury-Royal Exchange
42	W.Didsbury-Royal Exchange (in via Piccadilly)	1-12-1902	12-2-1939	West Didsbury-Royal Exchange
43	Greenheys (Claremont Road)-Piccadilly	3-4-1905	7-11-1937	Greenheys (Wilbraham Road)-Piccadilly

ROUTE		FIRST DAY	LAST FULL DAY AND ROUTE	
44	Moss Side-Stretford via Piccadilly	1-12-1902	6-7-1947	Southern Cemetery (Barlow Moor Rd)-Piccadilly
45	Chorlton-Piccadilly via Brooks' Bar	10-12-1910	5-12-1938	Piccadilly-Didsbury-Chorlton-Piccadilly
46	Chorlton-Piccadilly via Brooks' Bar	10-12-1910	22-11-1942	Chorlton-Piccadilly (as 46X from 6.12.1938)
47	Stretford Road-Chester Road via Piccadilly	1-12-1902	18-1-1931	Altrincham-Exchange in via City Road
48	Chester Road-Stretford Road via Piccadilly	1-12-1902	18-1-1931	Altrincham-Exchange in via Chester Road
49	Stretford (Barton Road)-Piccadilly	13-4-1903	18-7-1931	Sale Moor-Piccadilly
50	London Road-Deansgate-Whitworth Street circular	23-10-1905	29-3-1932	London Road-Deansgate via Whitworth Street
51	Oxford Road-Ardwick via Brunswick Street	1-4-1903	23-3-1940	Miller Street-Oxford Road
52	(Cricket & football services to Old Trafford)			
53	Cheetham Hill Road-Rochdale Road	16-7-1901	18-3-1930	Cheetham Hill Road-Brooks' Bar-Stretford Road
54	Chorlton-Albert Square via City Road	28-10-1921	20-3-1938	Southern Cemetery-Hightown (partly replaced by 37)
55	Queen's Park-High Street	5-7-1901	9-12-1934	Conran Street-High Street
56	(Services to M/c City F.C., Maine Road)			
57	Ashton-Denton via Guide Bridge (See 33)	23-7-1923	31-10-1936	Ashton (Bow Street)-Haughton Green
58	Chorlton (Barlow Moor Road)-Fallowfield	7-12-1924	17-7-1926	(Replaced by revised route 38)
58	Stretford-Pendleton (joint with Salford)	12-9-1926	16-1-1927	(Operated exclusively by Salford to 18-7-1931)
59	Mills Hill Bridge-Albert Square	24-3-1930	19-3-1932	Mills Hill Bridge-Cannon Street
77	Middleton Station-Victoria Bridge (ex-Salford route)	28-7-1930	19-3-1932	Middleton Station-Victoria Bridge

THE AUTHORS

TED GRAY is a Founder Member of the Manchester Transport Museum Society, and currently Honorary Secretary. For ten years he was also Secretary of the Greater Manchester Transport Society, in the period which led to the foundation of the Museum of Transport in Cheetham Hill. His boyhood passion was the tramways of the Salford area, but interest spread to include transport history of the surrounding townships. Previous publications include '*The Tramways Of Salford*', '*Trafford Park Tramways*', '*The Manchester Carriage & Tramways Company*', and two shipping books, '*A 100 Years Of The Manchester Ship Canal*' and '*Manchester Liners*'.

ARTHUR KIRBY has had a lifelong interest in Manchester tramways. He is the author of '*Dan Boyle's Railway*', the story of the early years of the Manchester tramway system, 1901-06, Dan Boyle being the first Chairman of the Tramways Committee. Arthur has also written '*Manchester's Little Tram*', an account of the single-deck trams on the 53 Circular Route, and '*Middleton Tramways*', the history of the Middleton Electric Traction Company, 1902-1925. He is a long-standing member of the Manchester Transport Museum Society, which operates a working tramway in Heaton Park, using a preserved 1914 Manchester single-deck tramcar. Arthur was the co-ordinator and project leader of the volunteers who embarked upon the five-year preservation programme, which resulted in a derelict vehicle being rebuilt and restored to splendid operational condition.

For a more detailed history of the Manchester tramways, the following publications may be consulted :-

Dan Boyle's Railway	—	*A.K.Kirby* (MTMS 1974)
Manchester's Little Tram	—	*A.K.Kirby* (MTMS 1964, 1979, 1990)
Middleton Tramways	—	*A.K.Kirby* (MTMS 1976)
The Manchester Tramways	—	*I.A.Yearsley* (Transport Publishing Co. 1988)

After the closure of the tramway system in 1949, the remaining standard cars were destroyed, but the 38 Pilcher cars had been offered for sale, and all found new owners elsewhere. Leeds borrowed one car or trial in 1946, and subsequently purchased it, along with six others 1948. The seven ex-Manchester cars continued to run in Leeds for another four years. Though painted in the livery of their adopted town, the unmistakeable outlines of the Pilcher cars rendered them instantly recognisable. This example is working on the Kirkstall Abbey route.

Other Pilcher cars went to Sunderland and Edinburgh, but the most northerly destination was Aberdeen, where R. Stuart Pilcher had started his managerial career. There the Corporation bought fourteen tramcars in 1947-48, said to have been selected from those in the be condition. Number 42 is in service on the Bridge of Dee route. As Leeds, the Manchester trolley pole was replaced by a bow collecto

In 1961 members of the Manchester Transport Museum Society discovered and purchased the hulk of single-deck tram car 765. This car, new in 1914, was withdrawn from service in 1930-31 after the closure of the 53 circular route. At that time many car bodies had been sold for use as garden sheds or caravans, and 765 had been languishing unprotected on a farm near Huddersfield. The body, in very poor condition, was moved first to Crich, site for the Tramway Museum in Derbyshire, and then to Manchester for restoration work to begin.

The subsequent project to recreate an operational tramcar from the remains of car 765 was long and difficult, but since 1979 the tram has been in Heaton Park, where a working tramway has been established in partnership with Manchester City Council. Members of the Society are now at work restoring a 1901 double-deck car, number 173, which, when complete, will also run in Heaton Park. The tramway operat on Sundays and Bank Holidays between Easter and October. T illustrations show the body of car 765 as found, being lifted on to low-loader for transportation to Manchester, and, as restored , ru ning in Heaton Park in 1981.

rams returned to Manchester in 1992 with the opening of the first hase of the Metrolink system, achieved by linking the former elec- ic railway routes to Bury and Altrincham with a short section of city entre street track, plus an extension to serve Piccadilly railway sta- on. The decision to utilise station platforms on the rail routes, led evitably to the adoption of high-access vehicles, a choice which present and future operators may regret. The trams, rails, bridge-work, street shelters, etc. were purchased abroad, which one critic likened to "importing umemployment." Only the electric motors and some signalling equipment have been manufactured in this country. Unit 1022 is passing through Sale station on the Altrincham line.

Unit 1017, St. Peter's Square, 1995. For tramcars which can be boarded only at high level, the street-running sections require ramps, steps, platforms and railings, together with associated paraphernalia. These unsightly features block pavements, require greater space and incur additional maintenace costs. Multiple unit operation quickly demonstrated that in the city centre all but the Piccadilly platforms were too short. The Market Street/High Street stopping points were reconstructed as one long island platform. The new line to Eccles (under construction 1999) will require similar provision along much of its length. For this route, land has been acquired compulsoril there has been lengthy and continuing disruption to road traffic, a incredibly expensive underpass is planned, and the town centr willbe spoiled. Yet, to be consistent, Metrolink might have made us of the former Manchester Ship Canal/LNWR railway line to Eccle Station, where there is ample room for a terminus on the former fou track site. It is revealed that vehicles designed for the Eccles line wi be incompatible with the existing system

MANCHESTER BUSES

A fascinating pictorial guide to the history
of the buses of Manchester

by
TED GRAY

On 6th of June 1981 members of Manchester Transport Societies held a combined event to mark the 80th anniversary of the 1901 inauguration of Manchester's electric tramways. Preserved vehicles stood side by side in Heaton Park. On the left is Tramcar 765, bearing a commemorative headboard, and to its right is Crossley 2150 one of the vehicles purchased to enable the conversion of Manchester's last tram route in 1949. Behind the Crossley are more former Manchester vehicles.

THE AUTHOR

For over 10 years, Ted Gray was Honorary Secretary of the Greater Manchester Transport Society, an organisation of transport enthusiasts. In 1978, with financial help from the Greater Manchester Passenger Transport Executive, the Society was able to establish the Museum Of Transport, which has a large display of preserved buses. Ted was also a founder-member, and remains Secretary, of the Manchester Transport Museum Society, which has a working tramway in Heaton Park. As well as preserving large exhibits, both Societies have extensive collections of archival material. Ted himself purchased and restored a former Salford bus, and, though now with new owners, this remains an exhibit in the Museum. Ted's professional career was in education, but he has always had an interest in transport history, and he is the author of several books and articles on local tramways and bus systems.

Acknowledgements

Students of Manchester Corporation's transport history can do no better than consult '*The Manchester Bus*' by **Michael Eyre** and **Chris Heaps** (Transport Publishing Company, 1989), which is a scholarly and definitive history of motor bus operations in the city. Earlier, in 1971, the same authors had produced '*Manchester's Buses.*' The amount of detailed research contained in those publications is comprehensive, and much information for this volume has been drawn from these works. The writer therefore acknowledges his deep indebtedness to the work of Mike Eyre and Chris Heaps. An equally-detailed companion work on the tramway system is '*The Manchester Tramways*' by **Ian Yearsley** (Transport Publishing Company, 1988). Acknowledgement is also made to the late G.R.(Ray) Dunning, who is remembered with gratitude by many historians for his obliging generosity and his inexhaustible search for illustrations of Manchester's transport history, a self-imposed task which provided a regular supply of 'new' pictures. Members of the Greater Manchester Transport Society have been most helpful.

The illustrations cover the period of municipal operation of local transport services, 1901-1969, and many hitherto unpublished pictures have been selected. Unless otherwise stated, the photographs are from the former Manchester Corporation Transport Department. Fortunately, these records were rescued and held in the safe custody of Ken Healey, then Depot Manager at Hyde Road Garage, to whom we are indebted for the preservation of much material of historical value.

Photo: Garside & Co., Barton Arcade

Between 1877 and 1901, horse-drawn tramcars of the Manchester Carriage & Tramways Company provided local transport services along most of the main roads radiating from Manchester's city centre to the outlying suburbs. From June 1901, Manchester Corporation began to provide its own services, as electric tramcars gradually replaced the Company horse-cars. The Chairman of the Manchester Tramways Committee was Daniel Boyle. (Boyle Street, at the side of the Corporation's first tram depot, was so named in his honour.) In 1906, when the municipal tramway system was still expanding, Daniel Boyle's colleagues must have been surprised to learn that he had accepted a position as Managing Director of a rival transport undertaking, the *Manchester District Motor Omnibus Company*. For five days, 1st-5th March 1906, the new Company offered free rides to impress specially-invited dignitaries. The sample journeys started from Albert Square, outside the Manchester Town Hall ! Regular services began in the southern suburbs on the 10th March, and the fleet grew to 18 in number. Despite ambitious plans, the Company passed into voluntary liquidation in October 1906. The Company's garage was in Westinghouse Road, Trafford Park, and the invitation card illustrated was that sent to Marshall Stevens, Managing Director of the Trafford Park Estates Company.

The Corporation's first venture with a motor bus was a brief trial of a Critchley-Norris open-top double-deck vehicle, which was not purchased. However, in 1906 an order was placed with Crossley Brothers of Openshaw for three motor buses with which to replace the horse-buses on the Northenden and Cheadle routes, districts where it had not been thought worthwhile to construct tramways. The three buses had Crossley engines in Leyland chassis (bearing 'Lancashire Steam Motor Company' maker's plates), with 33-seat bodies built by the United Electric Car Company of Preston, the tramcar-building firm. Number 3 (N 1602) was on the 2nd October 1906. Note the oil lamps, and the oil cans by the driving seat. The legal lettering records a maximum speed of 12 miles per hour; the 'N.15. C.G.3' indicates that the vehicle was licensed to operate in Northenden, Cheadle, and Gatley. The fluted Daimler-like radiator top was fitted by Leyland for only a short period.

MANCHESTER CORPORATION TRAMWAYS.

PALATINE ROAD

.. FOR ..

NORTHENDEN AND CHEADLE.

DURING the Summer Months at week-ends additional Cars are run between the CITY and PALATINE ROAD. 'Buses run regularly between Palatine Road and Northenden, and between Palatine Road and Cheadle.

Three Daimler chassis were acquired in 1915, and were fitted with 38-seat open-top bodies constructed in the Corporation's own workshops attached to Hyde Road tram depot, known as the 'Car Works.' Many more bus bodies subsequently originated there. NA 2687 was photographed at Longford Park on the Stretford-Chorlton service.

Two additional vehicles brought the bus fleet total to five by 1909, but in that year number 3 was converted to a tower wagon. The remaining four were withdrawn in 1913, when four new Daimlers with Dodson bodies were delivered. N 9247, seen here on the Northenden route, and its fellows lasted less than a year in service, for in 1914 two chassis were requisitioned by the War Department and the other two were adapted as tower wagons. The bodies were placed into store, to be used later on other chassis.

Pneumatic tyres came into general use in the mid-1920s, but were not originally fitted to six Bristol 'A'-type double-deckers delivered in 1927, and numbered 60-65. They were the first double-deck vehicles to have enclosed top decks. Number 65, photographed after the tyre change, illustrates the exposed staircase, which was outdated almost by the time of entering service. All six lasted until 1935. They had seats for 26 on each deck, total 52. The lower saloon of number 65 shows the patterned moquette seats, trimmed with leather.

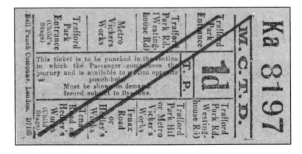

Accidents will happen! Bus 68, one of three 1927 Leyland 'Leviathan' vehicles, came to grief in May 1931, when it skidded and dropped on to the golf course at Northenden after braking sharply to avoid a cyclist. Numbers 66-68 were double-deck covered-top 52-seat buses, the first to be equipped with pneumatic tyres from the outset. Numbers 66 and 67 remained in service until 1934, but 68 was deemed irreparable and was converted into a breakdown crane, in which guise it lasted until 1958.

A rear view of bus 137 (VM 5320), an Associated Daimler chassis of 1928, shows the cut-away entrance of the Davidson 32-seat single-deck body. The Davidson factory was situated in Trafford Park, and there was strong support for local industry. The firm supplied bus bodies to Manchester and elsewhere over a six-year period before becoming a victim to the trade depression in the early 1930s.

When General Manager R. Stuart Pilcher decided in 1930 to convert the 53 route from tram to bus, 60 new low-bridge double-deck buses were purchased; 20 Crossley 'Condors' (numbered 189-208) and 40 Leyland 'Titans' (209-248). All had 'piano-front' bodies, supplied by five different makers. On the top deck, seats were arranged centrally in threes, with a sunken gangway at each side. In the lower saloon, the dropped gangways from above reduced the available headroom at the sides. (*Please Lower Your Head When Leaving Your Seat* was a familiar slogan.) However, height was retained for the central passageway. The term 'piano-front' referred to the characteristic curve, reminiscent of an upright piano. The first few months of bus operation on the busy and circuitous 53 route were characterised by a number of collisions. Leyland 217 (seen as towed into depot on 11th August 1931) was one of several vehicles damaged by collision with tram-way standards. In this case, the offending pole was struck after a skid in Dickinson Road. The open door behind the driver's cab is the emergency exit door.

A view of the Hyde Road Car Works on the 2nd December 1929. In the foreground is the area devoted to the construction of bus bodies, showing work well advanced on timber framing. In the centre, nearing completion, are bodies already mounted on the Crossley chassis of the 159-163 series, whilst in the background is the tramcar-body repair area. The oval rear window on the bus bodies was a distinguishing feature of the single-deckers in the 1929-30 period. After the brief flirtation with the 1906 buses, Crossleys had concentrated on motor car production at the Gorton factory, but by 1928 the firm was in financial difficulty, and sought opportunities in bus production. Manchester's wish to support local industry ensured the survival of the firm, and thus began a long and mutually beneficial association.

Photo: Daily Herald

Competition from independent 'pirate' omnibus operators reached a peak in the late 1920s. Goodfellow of Hyde was one such rival, and one of his grey and green Thorneycroft vehicles is seen in Wilmslow Road, Rusholme, on the service to Bramhall. Manchester tram 162, one of the replacement cars built in 1925, is on route 42 to West Didsbury. Note the tram's trafficator arm, a wooden board which could be swung outwards, useful for the driver at the front when turning left.

Lower Mosley Street Bus Station opened in 1928 to cater mainly for the long-distance or joint services. In this March 1931 view, an additional shelter is under construction (left). Tilling-Stevens buses of the North Western Road Car Company stand nearest the camera, with two Leyland 'Tigers' of Ribble Motor Services and Manchester Corporation beyond. Manchester buses worked from here, jointly with North Western, on the express service to Flixton.

Manchester's railway stations were constructed too late in the nineteenth century to be able reach the heart of the city. Instead, they formed a ring just outside the town centre, and so, for passengers changing trains, London Road Station (now Piccadilly) had to be linked by road services with Central, Exchange and Victoria Stations. On 24th October 1933, bus 172 (a 1930 Crossley) was on duty on route 62, linking Victoria and London Road Stations. Now, Metrolink trams perform the same duty.

The substitution of buses for trams in Stretford, Sale and Altrincham, led to substantial orders for more Crossley 'Condors,' this time with high-bridge 'piano-front' bodies. Number 280, one of 40 vehicles in the 279-318 series of 1931, is undergoing the tilt test. It has reached 29 degrees from the perpendicular, whilst carrying on the top deck 28 sacks, each filled with 10 stones of sand.

On the same day in 1933, buses 86 (on service 63 to Central Station) and bus 123 (the latter, lacking a route number box, departing for Victoria and London Road) were captured on the Exchange Station approach road.

A motor bus of the London & North Eastern Railway Company, apparently bearing two fleet numbers (187 on the front, 60 on the side), offered an alternative mode of travel to Sheffield as it waited for passengers at Victoria Railway Station in March 1931.

Parker Street Bus Station opened in 1931. Crossley 'Condor' 327, of the 'highbridge' piano-front design, waits to depart on service 49 to Sale Moor, whilst beyond may be seen an Oldham Leyland 'Tiger' (on the Greenfield service); a Goodfellow Thorneycroft; and Manchester 96, a 1927 Associated Daimler, on the Northenden service. Extreme left may be noted tramcars of Manchester and Stockport Corporations.

By mid-1932, the Parker Street passenger shelters had been constructed. In the foreground, Crossley 'Condor' 322 stands ready to depart on service 49c to Stretford (Barton Road), whilst 343 behind is on the full route 49 to Sale Moor. The bus station was extended to occupy the full width of Piccadilly in 1935.

Metro-Cammell provided a prototype all-metal body for 'Condor' 390 in 1932. An aluminium alloy frame, developed by Crossley in conjunction with Metropolitan Vickers of Trafford Park, was then used for 'Condors' of the 401-415 series of 1933. Here, bus 407 with panels removed, reveals its rear-end framework.

Substantial numbers of highbridge Crossley 'Condors' were acquired in 1931-33. The Hyde Road Car Works built many of the bodies, but others were purchased from Crossley, Hurst Nelson, and Strachan. Buses 320-389 were the last built to the 'piano-front' design. There were often detail differences from the various makers. Illustrated is bus 331, offering a rear view of the Strachan body. Note the board above the lower deck windows giving additional details of the route.

Changes for the new standard body design incorporated larger indicators on a sloping front. A Crossley 'Mancunian' with Metro-Cammell body, number 510, was one of several supplied in 1934, all of which remained in service until 1947-50. Supplementary destination details, illuminated at night, were held in a frame below the service number.

Problems caused by the timber frames of the 'piano-front' bodies led to the decision to commence a programme of fitting new bodies to the low-bridge vehicles. Bus 193, of 1930, gained its new body in 1935. Its original body (with a few others found to be in reasonable condition), was overhauled to be re-used on another chassis.

Queens Road Garage washing bays in 1935, showing bus 189, a Crossley 'Condor' of 1930 with a new body as fitted in 1934; and buses 466 and 477, both having the new standard body of 1934. Note that 466 carries a CONRAN ST. supplementary destination board. The ladders and platforms enabled the washing staff to reach top deck windows and roofs.

Two rear views of Crossley 'Condors' explain an ad-man's opportunity. Mason Advertising, noting that the rear window by the staircase was painted out *"for decency reasons"* (as on bus 448), tendered to use the space for 12-inch-high advertisement panels, to be stuck on the inside of the glass. Bus 412 outside the Queens Road washing shed, demonstrates the result. Later, in a doomed attempt to gain a new client for his agency, Mr.Mason made the tactical error of sending to rival Salford, a photograph showing the rear of a Manchester bus adorned with a toothpaste advertisement. Salford Transport Committee members had always refused to deface their vehicles with advertisements, and the Manchester picture was treated with scorn and derision, as being just the sort of thing *'they'* (i.e. Manchester) would fall for. Mason's offer to add over £400 per year to the Salford revenue was thus dismissed out of hand.

Piccadilly Bus Station as extended in 1935. Vehicles include Crossley 'Condor' 379 (left); Oldham Leyland 'Tiger' No.20, destination Greenfield; 'Condor' 282, on route 15A to Guide Bridge; and 'Mancunian' 423 on route 45 to Benchill. Five Manchester trams and one Stockport tram complete the picture.

A busy town terminus, yet hidden from the main Piccadilly bus station, was Stevenson Square, off Oldham Street, a spot somewhat difficult to find for anyone unfamiliar with the city centre. Here terminated several services from the northern and eastern suburbs. Crossley 'Mancunian' 516, new in 1935, waits to leave on service 25 to New Moston.

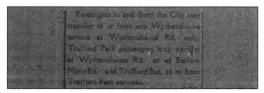

A shortage of vehicles in 1936-37 induced Manchester to accept a suggestion by which Metro-Cammell would supply bus bodies quickly, as long as some could be constructed to a standard design. Hence, the 546-601 series became two designs intermixed, some 'standards,' some 'streamliners.' All had a more informative route indicator layout. Bus 587 (DNB 43), new in 1937, was one of the last 'standards.'

The modernistic (for 1937) 'streamline' effect owed as much to the paint style as the body design. The windows on the new all-metal bodies were given rounded corners, and curves at front and rear. The new shape of the Crossley radiator (which retained the famous Maltese Cross trademark), and the deeper mudguards, were pleasing to the eye. In one version of the livery, the top-deck cream bands, swooped down to join the bands above the lower deck end windows, giving even more of a 'streamline' appearance (witness 670, under lift in Hyde Road Works). The front of bus 621 shows the revised destination display. The interior view of the lower saloon of bus 971 shows the Crossley name on the flywheel cowl, and some typically-Manchester body characteristics.

R. Stuart Pilcher, the Manchester Manager, anxious to convert the Ashton Old and New Road tramway routes to motor bus operation, reluctantly accepted a Council decision to run trolley-buses. This policy had been formulated on the argument that the city should use home-produced fuel, i.e. electricity from coal, rather than imported oil. A new depot, designed to accom— modate 115 trolley-buses, was constructed on Rochdale Road and opened on the 1st March 1938. In all, 76 vehicles were delivered in that year, 38 four-wheelers (1000-1037) and 38 larger six-wheelers (1050-1087). The depot interior view shows some of the four-wheel vehicles. Note the troughing holding the overhead wires. Six-wheeler 1055 at the garage exit shows the 'streamline' livery and the full front. Seventy-seven more trolleybuses (1100-1176) were ordered in 1939, which (providentially) helped to alleviate the wartime fuel shortage. Part of Hyde Road Garage was adapted to accommodate the additional vehicles.

The declaration of war in 1939 led to a fear of enemy air raids and the strict enforcement of blackout regulations. Headlamps were covered with masks, to allow only downward-pointing slits of light, and mudguards and fenders were painted with white paint, allegedly luminous, to show up in the dark. The white roofs were painted grey, so as not to be so easily visible from the air. Interior lighting was reduced to a minimum. Conductors issued tickets and gave change the dim light of a shaded battery lamp. Crossley 'Mancunian' 424, new in 1934, in Boyle Street, and 579, a 'standard' from the mixed batch of 1936, were both photographed as prepared for blackout conditions. 424 bears evidence of wartime scars, but 579 appears in good condition. ▶

◀ The new 963 shows one headlight only, in use, as at first required, the lamp having been removed from the nearest fitting.

Some single-deck buses were adapted for use as auxiliary ambulances, and most carried stretchers, lashed upright on the rear steps, as may be detected on buses 61 and 70, Leyland 'Tigers' of 1937-38 vintage. Bus 61 carries a front-window sticker, which reads *'Auxiliary Ambulance Stretchers To Hospital.'* In the severe winter of 1941, bus 70 carried out unusual duties whilst fitted with a snow-plough.

In 1940, fear of enemy air attack with poison gas, led to a series of decontamination practices, carried out in Hyde Road Yard. Under the supervision of Air Raid Precautions staff, bus 663 receives a thorough clean-down by personnel wearing protective clothing.

Between April 1940 and December 1942, in an experiment to combat the wartime fuel shortage, single-deck buses 50 and 51 were adapted to run on town gas. The gas was stored under pressure in a large bag, carried in a roof-mounted frame.

The departure of men to the armed forces led to the appointment of ladies to the hitherto all-male traffic staff. Conductresses were known as 'clippies,' a term derived from the task of clipping the tickets. By 1945, a total of 1591 conductresses were employed, together with 167 women cleaners and mechanics, and a few lady tram drivers. Their employment was terminated as male staff returned from war service.

In the period 1942-1944, Government instructions to conserve oil supplies led to some buses towing producer-gas trailers. The fuel was generated in a coke-burning device, which created fumes to be mixed with water vapour. The vehicles so converted proved to be under-powered, and suitable only for use on relatively flat routes. Although 84 trailers were allocated, Manchester was reluctant to use them, and only 20 buses were so adapted. Crews disliked the additional duty of stoking-up the fire. The trailer carried the warning, *'It is dangerous to open tuyere* (blast pipe) *door or use poker when engine is shut down.'* Trailer P202 is seen behind bus 467 at East Didsbury. The white-painted rings on the trailer were intended to make it visible in the blackout.

As the war progressed, supplies of Manchester's red and cream paint became difficult to acquire. The red-painted areas were more durable, so it was often the case that only the cream portions needed attention. These were often treated with more easily-obtainable shades of battleship grey.

As the threat of attack from the air receded, the 1939 lighting regulations were relaxed in September 1944 (when the blackout became a 'dim-out'), and cancelled altogether on the 23rd April 1945. It is reported that depot staff removed headlamp masks and interior lamp-shades from all service vehicles within 24 hours. Hyde Road Depot shows an unaccustomed glow as bus 137 (DNF 219), with headlamps blazing, passes the rows of trams whose interior lights illuminate the dark shed. The depot roof lamps await attention, and remain masked with portions of discarded destination blinds.

Part of Hyde Road Garage in 1945 shows a line of pre-war Crossley 'Mancunians,' with bus 485 (AVM 834) nearest the camera, its fleet number partially obscured by the cab's draught excluder. A later depot picture, evidently on a wet night, shows evidence of the 1945 'thousands' renumbering scheme, which allocated fleet numbers according to type. Thus, Crossleys added the numeral 2 as a prefix to existing numbers to be in the 2000 series; Leylands were in the 3000s; and Daimlers in the 4000s. Daimler 1295, GNA 443, new in 1940, became 4295 in 1946; whereas GNF 850, a new 1946 Crossley, was numbered 2920 direct into the new series. Wartime livery is still in evidence (right), and older vehicles appear on the left.

Photos: Daily Herald/News Chronicle

Buses 3227 (ex-227) and 869 (not yet renumbered) are seen in this 1948 view of Wilmslow Road.

A new use for old vehicles. Crossley 'Condor' 371, withdrawn from service in 1948, acts as a test load for staff working the mobile crane at the rear of Hyde Road Garage.

In the immediate post-war years, batches of new Crossleys, Daimlers and Leylands were added to the fleet, including in 1947 the first 8-feet wide buses, previous vehicles having conformed to the standard width of 7-feet 6-inches. The last tram route was converted to motor bus operation as from the 10th January 1949, and the arrival of large numbers of new vehicles facilitated the withdrawal of many of the older buses. The wider lower saloon of 3144, a 1949 Leyland 'Titan' PD1 with Metro-Cammell body, offered a few more inches to seated passengers. The uniformed guard is clipping tickets in a soon-to-be-replaced Bell Punch machine. Most of the 1949 Leylands remained in service until 1968-69, a total of some 19 years.

Photo: The Late R. F. Mack

The last Crossleys to be purchased were the 60 vehicles of the 2160-2219 series, delivered in 1949. By that date, the firm had been taken over by A.E.C. and the familar Maltese Cross trademark had been replaced on the radiator by the Crossley name. The new owners decided to cease the production of spares for Crossleys, thus curtailing the working life of many of the vehicles. Bus 2206 is seen in Piccadilly, waiting to leave on the 92 service to Hazel Grove.

Two joint cross-city services, numbered 57 and 77, were formed on the 15th January 1951 by joining Salford's routes to Swinton and Pendlebury with Manchester's routes to Reddish (Thornley Park and Bull's Head). At first, Salford Daimlers mixed with Manchester Crossleys on the new services, but the latter were removed with the arrival of Leyland PD2s 3330-3369 in 1953. Manchester 3337 stands at the Chorley Road, Swinton terminus of service 57 on 21st June 1955.

Another 38 four-wheel trolley-buses (1200-1237) were ordered in the post-war years, when the high tax on imported fuel made it worthwhile to consider electrical energy, in spite of the additional investment required in overhead wiring. The former tram route through Denton to Hyde, worked temporarily by motor buses, became a trolley-bus route (extended to Gee Cross) in 1950. A further 16 six-wheel trolleys (1240-1255) followed in 1951. Further extensions were contemplated at one stage, but the 62 new trolley-buses ordered for 1955 (1301-1362) were simply to maintain existing services and replace older vehicles. Indeed, the Moston routes were changed to motor bus operation, and Rochdale Road was converted to a bus garage in 1955. Numbers 1320 and 1354 are seen on the 218 and 216 services from Stalybridge. Trolley-bus operation ceased at the end of 1966.

After the demise of the Crossley empire, new vehicles in the 1950s were confined to Leyland and Daimler products. Bus 4419 (NNB 229), delivered in 1954, was a Daimler CVG6K model, with Gardner engine and Metro-Cammell 60-seat body.

THIS TICKET IS AVAILABLE ON ALL M.C.T.D. SERVICES IN THE MANCHESTER TRANSPORT AREA EXCEPT THE ALL NIGHT SERVICES AND SERVICE No. 90. ON THE JOINTLY OPERATED SERVICES THE MANCHESTER AREA TERMINATES AT THE POINTS SHOWN BELOW:—

SERVICES NOS.:—

25, 35X	Singleton Road	29,30,31,32,51,52	Cheadle (White Hart)
4	Bamford (Hall Gates)	18,20,20A,27,28,89,92	Lloyd Road
59	Mills Hill Bridge	74	Cheadle Green
17	Castleton Boundary	64	Park Road (Sharston)
2, 24	Moston Lane	91,222,223	Grosvenor Rd (Ashton Lane)
10,13,14,34,98	Hollinwood	36,37,38,39	Altrincham Bus Station
6, 216TB, 218TB	Snipe Inn	3,5,12,12A	King Street, Chester Road
127, 219TB	Guide Bridge	11, 23	Derbyshire Lane, Chester Rd.
21	Guide Lane	22	Longford Park
46	Edge Lane	56	Owler Lane
95,96	Victoria Bus Stn or Palatine Bridge	57, 77	St. Mary's Gate, (Deansgate)
		9, 16	Parrs Wood
125	Angel Street	15	Peter Street
210TB	Broomstair Bridge	58, 84	Trafford Park Entrance
33, 109	Bull's Head	109	Brooklands Rd (Altrincham Rd)

A picture to delight C. W. Baroth, the Salford Manager — a 1955 Daimler being towed around Hyde Road Depot by a fork-lift truck. It was alleged that Mr. Baroth kept prominently displayed in his office a picture of Manchester's 'bus-push,' a padded tractor-like vehicle, used to push-start reluctant buses.

The traditional radiator was specified by Manchester for its Leyland PD2s, but the days of the front-engined half-cab, rear-loading bus were drawing to an end when 3481 (TNA 481) arrived in 1958. Its 65-seat body was built by Burlingham of Blackpool. Within four years, the Department was taking delivery of its first full-fronted, rear-engined models.

Oh, dear! Bus 3697, standing on the inspection pits in 1969, was run into from the rear by another bus.

The ultimate in Manchester design, purpose-built for one-man operation. Bus 1001 of 1968 was a Leyland 'Atlantean' with a Park Royal body, designed for Manager Ralph Bennett by the Transport Department's own Ken Mortimer. The name *Mancunian* was chosen once again for this body style. The posters on the front were to inform passengers that fare payment was by coin-in-the-slot method. Certain modifications were made in the light of experience, but by the time the last 'Mancunians' had been delivered, the Transport Department had already been absorbed into the new SELNEC (South East Lancashire North East Cheshire) Passenger Transport Executive (later Greater Manchester Transport), which on the 1st November 1969 took over operation of eleven municipal transport undertakings. On that date the Manchester Transport Department ceased to exist.

The 1969 Passenger Transport Executive chose a livery of sunglow orange and cream, though it was some time before the majority of vehicles appeared in the new livery. Indeed, some were never re-painted, such as ex-Manchester 3419, new in 1956, which ended its days as a driver-training vehicle on the skid pan in Hyde Road Yard.

Photo: Ted Gray

Many ex-Manchester vehicles remained in service with the Passenger Transport Executive for a longer period than with their original owners. Here, bearing the new livery, ex-Manchester 3744, a 1965 Leyland 'Atlantean,' crosses Barton Bridge, Eccles, on service 22, after that had been re-routed via Patricroft to avoid the low canal bridge on Barton Lane. Alongside its fleet number, it displays the Birchfields 'BS' depot code. 20th May 1975.